ANCIENT EGYPTIAN WONDERS

Pharaohs of Egypt

Stuart A. Kallen

ReferencePoint Press®

San Diego, CA

LIBRARY OF CONGRESS CATALOGING-IN-PUBLICATION DATA

Kallen, Stuart A., 1955-
  Pharaohs of Egypt / by Stuart A. Kallen.
    p. cm. -- (Ancient Egyptian wonders series)
  Includes bibliographical references and index.
  ISBN-13: 978-1-60152-256-6 (hardback : alk. paper)
  ISBN-10: 1-60152-256-8 (hardback : alk. paper) 1. Pharaohs--History. 2. Egypt--Politics and
government--To 332 B.C. 3. Egypt--Civilization--To 332 B.C. 4. Egypt--Antiquities. I. Title. II.
Series: Ancient Egyptian wonders series.
  DT83.K25 2013
  932.01--dc23
                                                                                    2012000360

CONTENTS

A TIMELINE OF ANCIENT EGYPT

Editor's note: Dates for major events and periods in ancient Egyptian history vary widely. Dates used here coincide with a timeline compiled by John Baines, professor of Egyptology at University of Oxford in England.

Great Pyramids of Giza are built by Khufu, Khafre, and Menkaure.

First pyramid, the Step Pyramid at Saqqara, is built by Djoser.

Capital city of Memphis is founded.

Upper and Lower Egypt unify as one kingdom.

Late Predynastic Period (ca. 3100–2950 BC)

Early Dynastic Period (ca. 2950–2575 BC)

Old Kingdom (ca. 2575–2150 BC)

First Intermediate Period (ca. 2125–1975 BC)

Middle Kingdom (ca. 1975–1640 BC)

Hieroglyphic script is developed.

Old Kingdom collapses, resulting in a period of social upheaval and political chaos.

Egypt prospers during its classical period of art and literature.

Mentuhotep reunites Egypt.

Egypt enjoys peace for more than 50 years under Ramesses II, a noted warrior and prolific builder.

Ptolemy becomes king after Alexander's death in 323 BC; he founds a dynasty that rules Egypt for nearly three centuries.

The Rosetta stone, which later provides the key to deciphering Egyptian hieroglyphs, is carved.

Tutankhamun (King Tut) dies at a young age after a short reign; his undisturbed tomb is discovered in the Valley of the Kings in AD 1922.

Egypt regains its independence.

Hyksos rulers are driven from Egypt.

Persians conquer Egypt.

Hyksos kings invade and seize power in Egypt.

Nubians conquer Egypt.

Second Intermediate Period (ca. 1630–1520 BC)

New Kingdom (ca. 1539–1075 BC)

Third Intermediate Period (ca. 1075–715 BC)

Late Period (715–332 BC)

Greco-Roman Period (332 BC– AD 395)

Akhenaten introduces an unpopular monotheistic religion.

Alexander the Great conquers Egypt and makes it part of his vast empire.

Egypt is ruled by Hatshepsut, a woman pharaoh.

Cleopatra VII (better known as Cleopatra) serves as Egypt's last independent ruler.

Egypt becomes a province of the Roman Empire in 30 BC.

5

The Divine Ruler

In the long history of humanity, Egypt stands as the world's first nation. Around 3100 BC the pharaoh Narmer united Egypt into a single political and cultural entity. The degree of prosperity, poverty, and freedom experienced by ancient Egyptians was directly determined by the pharaoh, who controlled all land and resources. Unified under a single ruler, the Egyptians built the Great Pyramids of Giza, the Sphinx, and countless other temples and monuments that remain standing today as testaments to pharaonic power.

A LIVING GOD

The all-powerful pharaoh was perceived as the living embodiment of the gods and could take on many forms to smite his enemies. This is revealed in a slab of carved slate known as the Battlefield Palette, which was created in the thirty-first century BC. The palette portrays an unnamed pharaoh as a lion, trampling and ripping apart his enemies on a battleground. Other palettes from the era show the ruling pharaoh as a stinging scorpion, a charging bull, and even a catfish beating prisoners with a large stick. Egyptologist

> **DID YOU KNOW?**
> The word pharaoh is taken from the ancient Egyptian word *pr-aaa*, which means "great house" or "high house."

Toby Wilkinson explains the significance of these portrayals: "The message was clear: the king was not just a mere mortal who ruled by virtue of his descent and leadership abilities, he also embodied the strength and ferocity of wild animals, superhuman powers granted to him by divine authority."[1]

A stone sculpture of the pharaoh Khafre, with the falcon-headed god Horus behind his head, illustrates the majesty of the pharaohs and the belief that they were the living incarnation of Horus.

The soaring falcon is most closely associated with divine pharaonic authority. From the earliest days of Egyptian history, the pharaoh was believed to be a living incarnation of the falcon-headed god Horus, the supreme deity of the universe. Every pharaoh had several names, including a Horus name that symbolized the ruler's close relationship with the god. For example, the pharaoh Thutmose III, whose reign began around 1478 BC, was known as Horus Mighty Bull, Arising in Thebes.

Horus names provided a connection to the gods and served to elevate the pharaoh to impressive majestic status. The Horus name was practical as well. Someone who challenged the pharaoh's power was also picking a fight with the ruler of the heavens. This was seen as a reckless task that could lead not only to personal destruction but also to the annihilation of the entire universe.

The pharaoh was also seen as the earthly representative of the potent goddess Maat, who represented truth, balance, and justice. This gave pharaohs the power to direct the actions of all Egypt's priests, scholars, artists, soldiers, and scientists. These people, in turn, pioneered concepts in art, religion, medicine, philosophy, and agriculture that influenced civilization for thousands of years.

THIRTY-THREE DYNASTIES

The pharaonic system remained in place for about 3,100 years and encompassed 33 dynasties. Each dynasty consisted of three to 15 generations of related rulers. The use of the dynastic system in categorizing and classifying Egyptian history was devised by an Egyptian priest and historian named Manetho, who studied temple records around 300 BC. Manetho stated that Egyptian dynasties began during the "time of the gods"[2] and the creation of the earth itself. Although Manetho described an unbroken chain of all-powerful pharaohs, there were times of civil war and disunity when more than one person claimed to be ruler of the Egyptians.

The deeds of the pharaohs affected the people in Egypt and neighboring countries for more than 30 centuries. Even today millions of tourists flock to Egypt each year to gaze at the wonders of the ancient world created by and for the pharaohs. These monuments harken back to a time when Egyptians believed their land was ruled by the gods, who gave their orders to a single representative on earth—the pharaoh—who would rule the world forever.

The Founding Pharaohs

The ancient Egyptians believed that a pharaoh ascended into heaven upon death. There he spent eternity sailing across the sky in a small sacred boat called a bark. Every day the pharaoh would ride in his bark with the sun god Ra (also spelled Re), tracking the sun across the heavens from east to west. If the pharaoh chose to look down on Egypt from space, he would have seen an image resembling a brilliant green flower with its petals spreading out along the Mediterranean Sea. To the south of the petals, the pharaoh might have noticed a long green stem extending down to present-day northern Sudan. The flower and stem would have been surrounded by hues of golden and reddish brown.

In the twenty-first century, satellite images allow modern viewers to see the green flower-like image of Egypt taken from space. The green areas are created by the fields, gardens, and cities that thrive along the Nile River. The reddish-brown areas are the deserts that occupy most of the Egyptian territory, where little more than one inch (2.5cm) of rain falls annually.

During the fifth century BC, Greek historian Herodotus eloquently stated that "Egypt is the gift of the Nile."[3] Without its life-giving waters, the world's first nation-state would likely not have been born. The Nile is the world's longest river, winding 4,130 miles (6,647km) from central Africa to the Nile delta. The river runs through a wide valley for about 650 miles (1,046km), an area known as Upper Egypt because of its higher elevation. The land of Upper Egypt is divided between fertile irrigated fields along the Nile and towering cliffs that rise up to 1,500 feet (457m) above the river valley. The ancient Egyptians called the rocks and sand beyond the river *deshret*, or "red land." The word *desert* is derived from this term.

The cliffs end at modern-day Cairo, where the river blossoms into thousands of rivulets that form the large Nile delta, about 100 miles (161km) long and 155 miles (249km) wide. The Egyptians depended on the Nile to flood the delta, or Lower Egypt, every year. This left the land underwater for about 3 months, a period called inundation. When it receded, the river left behind fertile, dark soil known as *kemet*, or "black land."

THE UPPER KINGDOM

The people of the Nile were wandering hunters until around 4000 BC, when they first established small villages along the riverbanks of Upper Egypt. The hot desert climate and endless cycle of inundation allowed villagers to farm wheat, barley, and other grains as well as to raise goats, cows, and sheep. The plentiful food supply sustained a growing population.

By around 3500 BC, about 22 small towns and villages, called nomes, had been established in Upper Egypt. They were inhabited by people of the Naqada culture. One of the largest nomes, located about 50 miles (80km) south of present-day Luxor, grew to a city of 5,000 to 10,000 inhabitants by 3400

DID YOU KNOW?
The god Horus was often depicted as a falcon with its wings spread, perched on the neck of a pharaoh, whispering advice into his ear.

BC. The city was named Nekhen after the hawk god Horus. Today it is known by the Greek name Hierakonpolis, meaning "City of the Falcon."

Hierakonpolis was the first major metropolis built along the Nile, and it became a center for Egyptian culture. Modern archaeologists

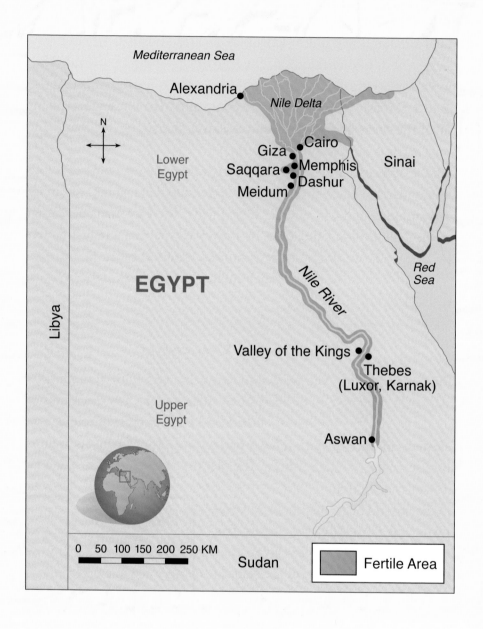

have discovered many examples of the beautiful arts and crafts created by the Naqada people. Skilled artisans made jewelry from ivory, lapis, and gold and created colorful, intricately decorated pottery. Production of these goods helped bring wealth to Upper Egypt and increased the power of Hierakonpolis.

What little is known about the rulers of Hierakonpolis can be found painted on the walls of brick-lined tombs created for nobility. In one tomb a wall painting shows a prince holding two lions; another painting portrays him vanquishing an enemy. These images represent power and hint that the rulers of Hierakonpolis engaged in wars with those living in smaller towns. Historians believe that by 3100 BC these battles were over and all of the nomes in Upper Egypt were united under a single king. Egyptologists refer to the period that followed as the Naqada Dynasty or Dynasty Zero.

Naqada tombs were also decorated with the first hieroglyphic alphabet, which consisted of stylized symbols representing plants, animals, buildings, tools, and religious rituals. This system of writing had a long-lasting influence, helping Egypt to grow into an advanced civilization. The highly complex system of communication also left modern historians with detailed records of ancient Egypt's long, rich history.

LOWER EGYPT

While cities grew in Upper Egypt, about 20 nomes were established in Lower Egypt between 3500 and 3300 BC. With the Nile delta underwater four months each year, people in the region were nomadic. They drove small herds of goats, cows, and sheep into dry regions during inundation and hunted and fished along the way. During the growing season they settled down in temporary structures to grow crops.

The tall marsh plant papyrus was an important resource for people in Lower Egypt. They used the plant to make paper, sandals, baskets, mats, boats, and other goods. The Lower Egyptians referred to their region as the Land of the Papyrus Plant. Whereas the wealth of the Upper Egyptians was based on gold, pottery, and precious stones, those in Lower Egypt prospered due to their location on the Mediterranean Sea. By 3100 BC the Lower Egyptians had established a thriving trade with people in neighboring Greece, Libya, Lebanon, Palestine, Persia, and Jordan. Maritime trade routes brought Lower Egyptians a steady supply of olive oil, timber, wine, cloth, and other goods on which they built a sophisticated culture.

MENI THE FOUNDER

The people of Upper and Lower Egypt shared a similar language and religious beliefs, but they clashed as the population grew in both regions. The people of Upper Egypt lived in a limited space between the fertile fields along the Nile and the tall cliffs that surrounded them. The princes in this region were organized, ruthless, and practiced at the art of war.

The people of Lower Egypt lived in a spacious area filled with abundant gardens, vineyards, and hunting grounds. Many were merchants and traders who had little reason to fight among themselves. However, the wealth of Lower Egypt made the region a tempting target for a hostile takeover.

Around 3100 BC a prince from Upper Egypt named Narmer set out to conquer Lower Egypt. It is unknown if he used political or military means, but Narmer is known today as Meni (also spelled Menes), "the Founder." He united the two lands of Upper and Lower Egypt and founded the First Dynasty.

Egyptologists only learned about Narmer through an accidental discovery. In 1898 two English archaeologists, James Quibell and Frederick Green, were looking for ancient treasures near the Temple of Horus in Hierakonpolis. The men were having little luck digging through the dusty ruins of the abandoned city when they discovered an intricately carved slab of stone.

> **DID YOU KNOW?**
> When the pharaoh Narmer united Upper and Lower Egypt into a single nation, the land was inhabited by about 200,000 people.

The carving, now known as the Narmer Palette, had elaborate pictures on both sides. One side of the palette shows Narmer wearing the Red Crown worn by pharaohs in Lower Egypt. He is looking down on a row of dead soldiers. Beneath the image, two hieroglyphic letters spell out Narmer's name using the symbol for catfish and another for chisel. The opposite side of the palette shows Narmer wearing the White Crown of Upper Egypt. Narmer is shown clutching an enemy with one hand while bashing

THE RIVER AND THE PHARAOH

The Nile River provided the ancient Egyptians with life-giving waters that allowed them to settle down and become farmers. But the Nile in its natural state was undependable as a source of irrigation. The founding pharaohs ordered the construction of a complex series of canals and dikes to make the Nile more reliable. In doing so they solidified their power and popularity. The dikes and canals built by the First Dynasty pharaohs channeled the river water into plots of farmland during the annual inundation. The abundant crops produced with this system provided sustenance to a growing population.

The Nile also provided the pharaohs with a means of policing Egyptian citizens. Since no one could survive more than a few miles distant from the river, Egypt's population was concentrated in the long, narrow river basin. The pharaoh's navy used the river to patrol the towns and villages up and down the long stretch of the river that linked the central government in Memphis with Egypt's outlying regions. With his powerful navy the pharaoh was able to monitor citizens' political and business activities while uniting dozens of cities, towns, and villages stretched out for hundreds of miles along the Nile.

his head with a club held in the other hand. A caption above the picture reads, "Pharaoh, the incarnation of the hawk-god Horus, with his strong right arm leads captive the Marsh-dwellers."[4] Egyptologists believe that the palette was created after Narmer united Upper and Lower Egypt into a single nation.

The ancient Egyptians regarded the unification of the two regions as the most important event in their history. This deed was equal to the creation of the universe in significance. It also demonstrated that the man responsible, Pharaoh Narmer, was an invincible god-king, both human and divine.

During his approximately 50-year reign, Narmer established a centralized government bureaucracy. He oversaw a phalanx of religious, economic, military, and political leaders. These officials carried out the pharaoh's orders with their own battalions of workers, which included soldiers, scholars, clerics, servants, and artisans.

AHA, THE FOUNDER OF MEMPHIS

Narmer was married to Queen Nihotep I, and their son, Hor-Aha, became the second pharaoh of a united Egypt sometime after 3100 BC. (Because of conflicting and missing ancient records, the exact dates of pharaonic rule in ancient Egypt are a matter of some debate among Egyptologists. This is especially true concerning events of the early dynasties.)

The name Hor is short for "Horus" and means "Fighting Hawk," but the pharaoh was often called Aha or was referred to by his Horus nickname, "the Fighter." One of Aha's most famous acts was founding the city of Memphis, which is just south of present-day Cairo. The pharaoh ordered the city built at the point where the Nile valley broadens out into the vast delta. This area was known by the ancient Egyptians as "the balance between two lands,"[5] the symbolic point of unification between Upper and Lower Egypt. However, the site of Memphis was

> **DID YOU KNOW?**
> Around 2800 BC Memphis had the highest concentration of workshops, warehouses, and businesses of any city in the world, and the port of Memphis was the central distribution point for food and merchandise for all of ancient Egypt.

originally a swamp. Aha ordered construction of a large dam to divert the Nile's waters away from the site. This provided reclaimed land for construction of the city.

Memphis grew into one of the greatest cities of the ancient world. It was home to Egypt's central government, lavish palaces of the pharaohs, imposing government buildings, cultural institutions, and verdant parks and gardens. Although little is left of Memphis today, it was the center of Egyptian power for more than 30 centuries.

Aha's name is recorded on a large stele, or slab of rock, known as the Palermo Stone, so named because it is in a museum in Palermo, Italy. The stele, found at the ruins of Memphis by an unknown archaeologist in 1865, lists the names of all the pharaohs of ancient Egypt from the First to the Fifth dynasties. According to the Palermo Stone, Aha reigned for 62 years. This means the pharaoh was very old when he was killed during a hunting accident, trampled to death by a charging hippopotamus.

Lily pads, lotus flowers, and papyrus plants grow in abundance along the Nile River, as depicted in this nineteenth-century illustration from a German encyclopedia. Papyrus was essential to the people of Lower Egypt, who used it to make paper, sandals, baskets, boats, and other items.

HUMAN SACRIFICE

Aha was buried in a simple brick-walled tomb. It was located in a sacred royal necropolis, or cemetery, called the precinct of Abydos. This burial ground, established by Narmer in the desert about 300 miles (483km) south of modern Cairo, was known as the land of the dead by the ancient Egyptians.

Aha's death probably created great stress among family members and administrators. During the First Dynasty, those closest to the pharaoh were sworn to serve him both in life and in death. This oath meant some of the pharaoh's wives, concubines, children, friends, and officials might be killed and interred with his mummified remains. Writer John Galvin describes what Aha's funeral procession in Memphis might have looked like:

> Led by priests in flowing white gowns, [Aha's] funeral retinue included the royal family, vizier [prime minister], treasurer, administrators, trade and tax officers, and Aha's successor, Djer. Just beyond the town's gates the procession stopped at a monumental structure with imposing brick walls surrounding an open plaza. Inside the walls the priests waded through a cloud of incense to a small chapel, where they performed cryptic rites to seal Aha's immortality. Outside, situated around the enclosure's walls, were six open graves. In a final act of devotion, or coercion, six people were poisoned and buried along with wine and food to take into the afterlife. One was a child of just four or five, perhaps the king's beloved son or daughter, who was expensively furnished with ivory bracelets and tiny lapis beads.[6]

Aha's tomb was first discovered by archaeologists in 2002. In addition to the six victims mentioned above, another 35 people were buried nearby. These additional burial sites, similar to those previously found around other royal tombs, are known as subsidiary or satellite graves.

The first satellite graves—those of later pharaohs—were discovered in Abydos in 1895. At that time archaeologists believed that the courtiers and family members in the graves committed self-sacrifice, killing themselves to accompany the pharaoh into the afterlife. In later years, however, advanced examination techniques like those used in police forensic labs showed that those who filled subsidiary graves were killed in grisly ceremonies. Some were poisoned, others were drugged and strangled or had their throats slit. Egyptologist Toby Wilkinson comments on this grim practice: "Egypt's early kings had the power of life and death over their subjects and did not hesitate to use it to demonstrate their own authority. . . . To be a member of the king's inner circle meant a life of fear."[7]

> **DID YOU KNOW?**
> The Red Crown of Lower Egypt—worn by the founding pharaohs—was adorned with a protruding curly wire that represented the long, slender, hairy tongue of the honey bee.

DJER SMITES HUNDREDS

Aha's son, Horus Djer, or "Horus Who Succors," was Egypt's third pharaoh. (*Succors* means "comforts or relieves.") Although the Palermo Stone says Djer ruled Egypt for 57 years, modern archaeologists put the number at 41 years. Whatever the length of his reign, Djer ruled a prosperous Egypt and expanded its borders during his life. In the earliest description of an Egyptian military maneuver, an ancient papyrus text describes one period of Djer's rule as "the Year of Smiting the Land of Stjt." It is believed that this references the Egyptian invasion of Palestine and Syria.

The Egyptian sciences flourished during the time of Djer, who was later described as a great physician. The Egyptian priest and historian Manetho claimed the pharaoh wrote about anatomy and disease in a medical papyrus still in use thousands of years after his death.

Djer might have been a healer while alive, but his death set a record for human sacrifice. Djer's tomb at Abydos was surrounded by 338 subsidiary graves. Evidence of mass murder was found among

Gods and Kings

The Egyptians were united in their complex religious beliefs before they were united as a nation. When the early pharaohs founded the First Dynasty, they convinced average Egyptians that their rulers were working hand in hand with the gods. The ancient Egyptians were polytheistic, meaning they worshipped many gods and goddesses. The Egyptian pantheon consisted of hundreds of major deities and thousands of minor ones, both male and female. Egyptians believed the pharaoh was the son of the sun god Ra, represented as a male figure with a ram's head. The god of the Nile, called Hapi, Hep, or Hepi, was nearly as important as Ra. The male god is represented with large, pendulous breasts and a fat belly. This image symbolizes the life-giving bounties of the river. The pharaoh was thought to work alongside Hapi to provide water, food, and a successful annual inundation.

Osiris was the god of the afterlife, represented as a mummy with a king's crown on his head. The pharaoh was believed to become Osiris after death. Osiris's sister and wife, Isis, was the queen of the gods. Isis was represented by a female figure on a throne.

the remains. One etching on a fragment of ivory shows a man kneeling down with his arms tied behind his back. Another man stands before him holding a knife, ready to plunge it into the victim's heart. In the other hand the knife-wielding character holds a basin to catch the blood. In another gruesome discovery, a piece of a woman's arm was found still wearing four bracelets made from gold decorated with amethyst, turquoise, and lapis beads. The arm likely belonged to one of the pharaoh's concubines.

A FLOWERING OF CULTURE

After Djer's death circa 3008 BC, his son Djet ruled for about 20 years. Little is known about his life, but 174 subsidiary graves were found around his tomb. The tomb of the next pharaoh, Den, had a similar number of graves. Den ruled for about 40 years, and his chief accomplishment was inscribed on a piece of ivory in his tomb. The image shows Den with his mace raised high before a foreign chieftain. The inscription reads, "The first time of the smiting of the East."[8]

Three more pharaohs ruled briefly after Den, bringing the First Dynasty to an end in 2890 BC. Together the pharaohs of the dynasty smote their enemies and expanded their nation's borders. For reasons unknown, human sacrifice ended abruptly at the end of the First Dynasty. Wilkinson offers a theory as to why this practice was stopped: "[Eliminating] an entire entourage at the end of each reign was hugely wasteful of talent, and the ancient Egyptians were nothing if not practical."[9]

> **DID YOU KNOW?**
> The bodies of early pharaohs were placed in wooden coffins in the fetal position, with the head bent forward and the limbs drawn up. A funerary meal was placed in front of the pharaoh's face to provide nourishment in the afterlife.

Beyond human sacrifice, the rulers of the First Dynasty oversaw the flowering of Egypt's intellectual, artistic, scientific, and administrative traditions. The cultural institutions established by the founding pharaohs would remain at the heart of Egyptian civilization for another 3,000 years.

CHAPTER 2

The Monument Builders

In 1903 English archaeologist Flinders Petrie was digging in the ruins of the ancient necropolis at Abydos. He came upon a small headless statue that fit into the palm of his hand. The name on the ivory carving read "Khufu." Petrie knew that Khufu was the pharaoh credited with building the Great Pyramid of Giza, one of the wonders of the ancient world. No image of Khufu had ever been found, and Petrie halted all work at the Abydos excavation until the head of the statue could be located. Crews sifted through the sands of the necropolis for three grueling weeks until they discovered the head from Khufu's statue.

It is one of the ironies of history that the only representation of Khufu, the man responsible for the building of the Great Pyramid of Giza, is a 3-inch-tall (8cm) statue, now on display at the Egyptian Museum in Cairo. Khufu came to power around 2551 BC. His pyramid rises 481 feet (147m) above the desert floor and has a square base that is 756 feet wide (230m) on each side. The Great Pyramid contained more masonry than any other structure on earth for more than 4,400 years, until the Hoover Dam was completed on the Colorado River in AD 1935.

Khufu was a pharaoh of the Fourth Dynasty during an era known as the Old Kingdom. The Old Kingdom lasted from about 2575 to 2150 BC. During the Old Kingdom, Egypt was governed by pharaohs from the Fourth through Eighth dynasties, and Egyptian culture was stable and highly developed. Advances from previous centuries in the arts, hieroglyphic writing, agriculture, and science reached new heights of sophistication. Nowhere was this more obvious than in the fields of architectural design and building technology, which resulted in two centuries of pyramid construction unique in human history.

This ivory statuette of Khufu, the king who built the Great Pyramid at Giza, was discovered by English archaeologist Flinders Petrie in 1903. It is the only known representation of the Old Kingdom ruler.

MAKING A MUMMY

When a pharaoh died, his body was taken to an embalming workshop, called a *wabt*. There, one group of priests conducted religious ceremonies while another went to work with embalming tools. The intestines, liver, lungs, stomach, and other internal organs were removed and stored in special clay containers called canopic jars. After this process, the body cavity was carefully washed and rinsed with spices and palm wine.

The next step of mummification required the priests to completely dehydrate the body. This was done with a natural salt, call natron, which was heaped upon the cadaver and left for a period of 40 days. Natron left the corpse shriveled, shrunken, and black. To fill in the body cavity to natural proportions, the priests filled it with sand, sawdust, or linen rags. For the final step, the chief priest took hundreds of feet of linen strips and carefully wrapped them around the entire corpse. Small magic objects, such as jewels and amulets, were placed between the layers of the linen. This last process took about 15 days to complete. When the wrapping was finished, a red burial shroud was wrapped tightly around the body. A lifelike mask was placed over the face so the gods would recognize the face of the dead pharaoh.

RELIGIOUS MONUMENTS

The pyramids were massive government work projects that required hard labor by tens of thousands of average citizens. These workers were not motivated by financial rewards. Money did not exist in ancient Egypt. The pyramid builders were performing a sacred duty, creating glorious religious monuments for their pharaohs out of the rocks of the desert.

The construction of elaborate pyramid tombs during the Old Kingdom was driven by ancient writings appropriately named the Pyramid Texts, which were written on papyrus scrolls around 2400 BC. The texts say that each person has three vital life forces: the physical body and two nonmaterial elements called the *ka* and the *ba*. The *ka* was a universal life force that extended back through previous generations to the gods. The *ba*, comparable to the Western concept of the soul, was unique to each individual.

When someone died the Egyptians believed it was necessary to turn the remains into a mummy so the *ka* would have a place to stay. During the Old Kingdom era the time-consuming, specialized mummification process was performed only on the pharaoh, his family, and very important officials.

When the pharaoh died, his *ba* and his *ka* were reunited with his mummy in a special ceremony at his pyramid. At this point the sun god Ra took on great importance. Ra was an eternal and renewable force that spent the day traveling across the sky and the night tracking across the underworld ruled by Osiris. Ra's daily birth, death, and rebirth were the pattern for the pharaoh's life, death, and resurrection. Many Egyptologists believe the pyramids were built to act as ramps that allowed the pharaoh's *ba* to launch into the sky, where it could join Ra.

DJOSER'S STEP PYRAMID

The pyramidal launching pad theory is unproved, but pyramid building was central to Egypt during the Old Kingdom. Pyramid construction began just before the start of the Old Kingdom, with the Third Dynasty king Djoser. He ordered the Step Pyramid constructed at Saqqara, northwest of Memphis. This towering structure, visible from a distance of 20 miles (32km), served as a model for the pyramids built at Giza about a century later.

Before Djoser, the remains of pharaohs were placed in structures called mastaba tombs. These were simple flat-roofed, rectangular structures with burial chambers located deep below ground. Djoser's Step Pyramid was constructed from six large mastaba-like structures of diminishing size, piled one atop the other. Unlike regular mastabas, which were made from mud bricks, the Step Pyramid was constructed from limestone carved from a nearby cliff. The pyramid was designed by the great architect Imhotep, who oversaw its construction. Today the name Imhotep is as well known among scholars as those of the pharaohs for whom the monuments were built.

DID YOU KNOW?
The Step Pyramid measures about 358 by 411 feet (109 by 125m) at its base and rises to a height of nearly 203 feet (62m). It was the first building ever constructed with cut stone masonry.

Like many ancient pharaohs, little is known about Djoser beyond clues found in his burial chamber. The Step Pyramid is honeycombed with shafts, tunnels, and passageways. The only remnant of Djoser is his mummified left foot. However, within one of the hallways a large limestone statue shows the seated figure of Djoser wrapped in a long white cloak. Displayed today in the Egyptian Museum, this is the oldest known life-size royal statue. Another depiction of the pharaoh is a raised image carved into the limestone in a sculptural style called relief. It shows Djoser wearing the tall White Crown and a ritual false beard. He is taking part in the Heb Sed festival, an ancient ceremony that celebrated the continuing rule of a pharaoh. In this relief Djoser is running to affirm that he is fit, healthy, and powerful.

A NEW TYPE OF GOVERNMENT

Djoser ruled for 19 years, a relatively short period considering his accomplishments. As Egyptologist Peter A. Clayton states, "This scarcely seems long enough for the construction of a monument as remarkable as the Step Pyramid, but it is powerful testimony to the authority of the king. To build such a structure would have required a vast workforce, not to mention a strong government to organize and feed the workers."[10]

To accomplish the monumental building project, Djoser created a new type of government. Unlike previous pharaohs who gave royal relatives great powers, Djoser appointed a group of professional administrators who worked within a structured bureaucracy. These people were drawn from all levels of Egyptian society and were hired for their skills and organizational talents rather than their connections to the court. Djoser's lieutenants managed teams of mathematicians, designers, artists, masons, woodworkers, haulers, sailors, cooks, cleaners, and countless others needed to coordinate construction. Toby Wilkinson notes that the pharaoh's new type of administration changed the nation: "As Egypt embarked on pyramid building, the pyramids built Egypt. . . . It was a pattern of advancement that would be followed for many centuries to come. From now on, the history of ancient Egypt would be made by private individuals as well as their royal masters."[11]

The Old Kingdom pharaohs built massive pyramid-shaped tombs to assure their journey into the afterlife. Thousands of workers toiled on the pyramids. Among them were masons (pictured) who prepared limestone blocks for pyramid construction.

SNEFERU, "LORD OF THE UNIVERSE"

Pyramid construction and design took another great leap forward after the pharaoh Sneferu founded the Fourth Dynasty that ushered in the Old Kingdom. Sneferu's Horus name was Neb-maat. In its basic translation the term *neb* means "lord," and *maat* means "truth." However, translating Sneferu's Horus name to mean "Lord of Truth" does little justice to the actual meaning of the words as understood by the ancient Egyptians.

The word *neb* signified not only "lord" but also "possessor" and "owner." The goddess Maat was understood to be the deity who regulated the stars, the seasons, and the actions of all mortals, gods, and goddesses. Maat brought order to the universe from the chaos that reigned at the beginning of creation. To be the lord and owner of the wisest, most powerful force in the entire universe was quite a claim, even for a pharaoh. As Wilkinson explains, "Sneferu was announcing nothing less than a new model of kingship. For him, the exercise of power was no longer confined to dispensing justice. It meant having a monopoly on truth. The king's word was the law because the king himself was the law. If this smacked more of divine than human authority, that was the point."[12] Sneferu also gave himself a new, nontraditional name: Netjer Nefer, or "the Perfect God."

> ## DID YOU KNOW?
> The official title of the Step Pyramid's architect, Imhotep, was "the Chancellor of the King of Upper and Lower Egypt, Administrator of the Great Palace, Hereditary Lord, Greatest of Seers, Imhotep, the Builder, the Sculptor, the Maker of Stone Vases, Chief of that Which Heaven Brings, Earth Creates and the Nile Brings."

A NEW VISION OF THE FUTURE

If the number of pyramids attributed to one pharaoh is any proof, Sneferu was the most powerful king in Egypt's history. He used his total control of government and society to build three major pyramids and perhaps two smaller ones. He chose the site of Meidum (also

THE GREAT SPHINX

The Great Sphinx of Giza was carved out of the limestone rocks in front of the pharaoh Khafre's pyramid sometime during his reign. The statue, with the head of a man and the body of a lion, is 241 feet (73m) long and 20 feet (6m) wide. With the top of its head rising 66 feet (20m) above the desert floor, the Sphinx is about the size of a modern six-story building.

Egyptologists believe the Sphinx was constructed to guard and protect the pyramids of Giza. The ancient Egyptians likely called the Sphinx *seshepankh*, which means "living image." This is interpreted to mean the statue is the living image of Khafre or possibly the ancient sun god, Atum. Some archaeologists, however, believe the face on the Sphinx is modeled on Khafre's younger brother and successor, the pharaoh Djedefre, who might have been responsible for its construction. Whatever the case, it is estimated that it took 100 workers with primitive stone tools more than three laborious years to carve the Great Sphinx out of the living desert rock. Whoever ordered its creation was undoubtedly viewed as a god-king by the Egyptian artisans, whose work stands today as a reminder of the power of ancient pharaohs.

spelled Maidum) for the first pyramid, and this location had its own symbolism. Until Sneferu founded the Fourth Dynasty, pharaohs were buried in the ancient cemeteries at Abydos and Saqqara. When Sneferu built a seven-step pyramid at Meidum, 35 miles (56km) south of Saqqara, it was a break with long-standing traditions.

The evolution of the Meidum pyramid also shows a new vision of the future. At first the monument was a seven-step pyramid that resembled Djoser's Step Pyramid. Sneferu later added another step, raising the height of the pyramid to 306 feet (93m). This made it more than 100 feet (30m) taller than Djoser's tomb.

After construction at Meidum, the pharaoh moved his royal headquarters from Memphis several miles to the southwest to Dahshur. There, within sight of Djoser's pyramid, Sneferu ordered construction of a monument he called Appearance, which translates as "Rising Sun." In the original design, this pyramid did indeed rise toward the sun with walls built at an incredibly steep angle of 60 degrees, towering to a commanding height of 500 feet (152m). Despite Sneferu's claims of divinity, the Lord of the Universe could not overcome the forces of gravity. About halfway through construction, the Appearance pyramid began to crack and crumble as the ground underneath sank from the weight of the stones. When the internal hallways, stairs, and burial chamber threatened to cave in, 40 ships full of pine logs were imported to hold up the walls.

> **DID YOU KNOW?**
> Ancient Egyptians associated beards with divinity, and during celebrations and public appearances pharaohs wore long, wavy, pointed false beards that were attached to the ears by string.

Facing an emergency, architects were forced to shore up the outer walls of the pyramid with large blocks, reducing the angle to 54 degrees. To finish the top third of the pyramid, the angle was reduced further, to 43 degrees. Rather than create what the ancient Egyptians would have called a gleaming pyramid, Sneferu was left with what is now known as the Bent Pyramid. This would never do as a final resting place for the man who called himself the Perfect God.

THE RED PYRAMID

Architects used the lessons from this failure and began work on the Red Pyramid, so named because of its rust-hued limestone blocks.

Djoser (pictured) built the predecessor to the Giza pyramids. Known as the Step Pyramid, it consisted of six levels, each one smaller than the one below it, and an underground burial chamber.

However, Sneferu was 20 years into his reign by this time, and it was feared that he would soon die. To ensure that the pharaoh would have a proper tomb, workmen returned to the Meidum step pyramid. Using techniques learned on the Bent Pyramid, they refashioned the step pyramid into a true pyramid by filling in the steps with stones and covering them with a fine white limestone casing.

Egyptologists estimate that the Red Pyramid was completed in about 10 years. At a height of 341 feet (104m), it was a fitting monument for Sneferu. The pyramid could be entered by a descending corridor that ended at two rooms with 50-foot (15m) vaulted ceilings that served as burial chambers.

Sneferu must have commanded nearly every able-bodied worker in Egypt. While laborers built three pyramids at the same time, Sneferu also constructed fortresses, palaces, temples, and two smaller pyramids. When the pharaoh died he was most likely buried in the Red Pyramid. Sneferu's mummy has never been found, and like Khufu, only one eroded statue of the pharaoh remains.

THE GREAT PYRAMID

Khufu was Sneferu's son, and by the time he came to power, the human and material resources necessary for pyramid construction were already in place. Egyptologists estimate it took 10,000 to 20,000 workers more than 20 years to build Khufu's Great Pyramid. To do so they had to move 2 million stone blocks with an average weight of around 2.5 tons (2.3mt). The largest blocks were up to 70 tons (64mt), and some were dragged from quarries 500 miles (805km) away. To this day the exact methods used to construct the Great Pyramid remain unknown. The ancient Egyptians had no modern equipment, such as steel cables, pulleys, power tools, trucks, or cranes, yet every stone on the Great Pyramid was put in place with a striking degree of accuracy.

The interior of the pyramid was as carefully planned and stunningly executed as the exterior. Corridors were lined with granite stones that weighed more than 30 tons (27mt) each. Other walls were covered with beautiful white and red limestone. The King's Chamber, probably meant to be the final resting place for Khufu, contained a large sarcophagus—known as the Granite Coffer—hollowed out from a single block of solid red granite. How the Egyptians expertly cut this hard stone with primitive tools remains unknown.

After the pyramid was completed, it was surrounded by a limestone wall 26 feet (8m) high. Two buildings called mortuary temples were constructed in the courtyard along with beautifully carved columns, statues, steles, and temples. These were all part of a mortuary complex where Khufu, his wives, and his children were believed to be mummified. The mortuary complex was also used as a sacred space where the pharaoh's followers and relatives could continue to honor him and present him with presents, food, and drink during his afterlife.

LITTLE IS KNOWN ABOUT KHUFU

Despite his grand funerary monument, Egyptologists have never found evidence that proved Khufu was laid to rest inside the pyramid. There are no traces of embalming materials or linen that might have come from a mummy. And little is known about the pharaoh. Various ancient inscriptions say he led military raids into the Sinai, Libya, and the nation of Nubia, located in what is now southern Egypt and northern Sudan.

It is known that Khufu was at the center of a funerary cult that lasted 2,000 years after his death, finally ending with the fall of the Twenty-Sixth Dynasty sometime around 525 BC. Egyptian funerary cults were based on religious practices and teachings that centered on the afterlife of a deceased pharaoh. Those who worshipped in the Khufu cult did so at the funerary complex at the Great Pyramid and likely believed he would answer their prayers and use supernatural powers to improve their lives.

> **DID YOU KNOW?**
> The 30-ton (27mt) granite stones in the King's Chamber of the Great Pyramid of Giza are so perfectly joined that a knife blade will not fit between the cracks.

One of the earliest descriptions of Khufu's reign was written by the Greek historian Herodotus around 443 BC, about 2,100 years after the pharaoh's death. Herodotus called Khufu by his Greek name, Cheops, and compared him unfavorably to his father. Herodotus wrote that whereas Sneferu created a perfect state of justice across Egypt, Cheops was a wicked tyrant: "Cheops became king over them, and brought them to every kind of evil: for he shut up all the temples, and having first kept them from sacrifices there, he then bade all Egyptians to work for him."[13]

UNIFICATION WITH THE SUN GOD

Khufu died as the finishing work was being completed on the Great Pyramid. Khufu's son, the pharaoh Khafre (also spelled Khafra), built a slightly smaller pyramid next to Khufu's, which originally rose to a height of 474 feet (144m). Khafre, who reigned for more than 25 years, is also believed to have built the Great Sphinx to stand guard in front of his pyramid and provide it with protection. The Great Sphinx is the largest freestanding sculpture in the world. This giant stone monument has the body of a lion and the face of a man. Many Egyptologists believe the face is that of Khafre and the sphinx symbolizes his unification with the god Atum, who appears in the form of a lion.

The third pyramid at the Giza complex was built by Menkaure, Khufu's grandson, whose reign began toward the end of the Old Kingdom's Fourth Dynasty. With about 10 percent of the mass of his grandfather's Great Pyramid, Menkaure's tomb is 335 feet by 343 feet (102 by 105m) and rises to a height of around 213 feet (65m). Historians believe the construction of pyramids for Khafre and Khufu exhausted much of Egypt's material and human resources. This made it impossible for Menkaure to build a pyramid equal in size to those of his predecessors.

> **DID YOU KNOW?**
> A ceremonial wooden boat was sealed in a pit at the base of the Great Pyramid so Khufu's soul could sail into the afterlife.

The pyramid age drew to a close as the Fourth Dynasty ended around 2450 BC. Never again would pharaohs command the nation's workforce and natural resources to create monuments to themselves on such a grand scale. While little else is known about the reigns of Khufu, Khafre, and Menkaure, today their massive pyramids at Giza attract around 8 million tourists a year. And their stairways to the sun from the desert floor are eternal monuments to the powers that Ra, Maat, and Horus held over the ancient Egyptians and their god-kings.

CHAPTER 3

Pharaohs of the Golden Empire

On November 26, 1922, the British archaeologist Howard Carter removed a large stone door from a royal tomb in the Valley of the Kings near present-day Luxor, Egypt. The barrier had protected the tomb of the Eighteenth Dynasty pharaoh Tutankhamun since about 1323 BC. Carter pushed a small electric light into the four-room tomb and, as he later wrote, "I was struck dumb by amazement."[14] King Tut's tomb was packed with a jumble of priceless treasures. They included the pharaoh's mummy and the bejeweled containers that had been holding his mummified remains for more than 3,000 years. Tutankhamun's body was set in a solid gold coffin, and his face was covered with a gold death mask.

Other items found in Tut's tomb—meant for his use in the afterlife—included gold jewelry, luxurious furniture, sandals, necklaces, mirrors, slippers decorated with gold, linen loincloths, and 27 pairs of embroidered gloves. Tutankhamun was buried with 30 large jars of vintage wine and hundreds of other items, including chariots, statues, game boards, 130 walking sticks, dozens of bows and arrows, boomerangs, and knives.

Tutankhamun was only a boy when he ascended to the throne circa 1334 BC. Egyptologists think he died about 10 years later, possibly from sickle-cell disease or malaria. Today the boy-king is one of the most famous rulers of Egypt thanks to the thousands of possessions discovered in his tomb. Beyond that, Tutankhamun's historical deeds were few. As Carter put it, "[We] might say with truth that the one outstanding feature of [Tut's] life was the fact that he died and was buried. Of the man himself . . . and of his personal character we know nothing."[15]

MOUNTAINS OF GOLD

King Tut came to power during a period known as the New Kingdom, which began around 1539 BC and lasted nearly 500 years. During about half of the New Kingdom era, Egypt was controlled by pharaohs of the Eighteenth Dynasty, who were the wealthiest in ancient Egyptian history. The pharaohs ruled a huge empire and collected

British archaeologist Howard Carter and his patron Lord Carnarvon gaze at the tomb of King Tutankhamun. King Tut (as he came to be known) came to power during Egypt's New Kingdom, a period characterized by pharaohs who possessed great wealth and wide-ranging powers.

mountains of gold that paid for glorious monuments, towering statues, and spectacular works of art. The power and glory of the New Kingdom was such that even a minor pharaoh like King Tut was surrounded with stunning opulence, even in death.

Eighteenth Dynasty pharaohs created a military superpower unlike any in previous ages. They led armies into neighboring lands and conquered their enemies. Foreign capitals were plundered for their wealth, and the riches propelled Egyptian culture to towering heights.

GOD-KINGS AND MILITARY HEROES

Before the rise of the New Kingdom, the people of Egypt lived through a two-century era called the Second Intermediate Period. During that time, Egyptians were subjugated, enslaved, and oppressed, ruled by despised foreigners of Syrian heritage called the Hyksos, who were aided by Nubian allies. A war for liberation began around 1574 BC and raged for several bloody decades. The Hyksos were finally ejected by the Egyptian war hero Ahmose I, who became the first pharaoh of the Eighteenth Dynasty.

In order to prevent another foreign occupation, Ahmose I led an army into the Hyksos-controlled Canaan territory, located in present-day Israel and Lebanon. The victories of Ahmose I set Egypt on a new course. For the first time in its long history, the nation was governed as a military state. Ahmose and other pharaohs of the Eighteenth Dynasty were not only revered as god-kings but hailed as military heroes as well.

With the borders secured and the enemy banished, there was a renaissance in art. Ahmose dedicated one-tenth of all Egyptian resources to the worship of the gods and goddesses, which resulted in a massive increase in temple and monument construction. Cedar wood was imported from Lebanon and Tura limestone from Canaan. The center of the building activity was Thebes, an Upper Egyptian city about 400 miles (644km)

DID YOU KNOW?
Amenhotep I's royal names, "Bull Who Conquers the Lands" and "He Who Inspires Great Terror," were chosen to frighten Egypt's foreign enemies.

south of Giza. Ahmose moved the government to Thebes while the old capital, Memphis, remained the chief headquarters for the military.

THE PLACE OF TRUTH

Ahmose died around 1514 BC and his son, Pharaoh Amenhotep I, decided to create a new burial site for royalty. Amenhotep saw that the elaborate pyramid tombs of previous pharaohs had been desecrated and plundered by grave robbers. In order to ensure himself and his descendants a peaceful afterlife, Amenhotep divided the royal burial process into two parts: one public, the other very private. For the public, Amenhotep constructed huge mortuary temples where his funerary cults could worship him for eternity. The burial process, however, was held in secret. The mummified remains of New Kingdom pharaohs were interred far from the public eye, in a necropolis created by Amenhotep called the Valley of the Kings. This elaborate warren of underground tombs was built within the inaccessible cliffs on the west bank of the Nile, opposite Thebes.

The construction of the necropolis at the Valley of the Kings was a well-guarded secret. The only people who knew about the burial site lived in a village called the Place of Truth, located in a remote valley in the Theban hills. The Place of Truth was filled with workers and artisans who dug the burial chambers, constructed the tombs, and created the luxurious artwork and crafts entombed with the deceased pharaoh. For more than five centuries the builders and artisans who lived in the Place of Truth were sworn to secrecy; punishment for revealing their work was death.

> **DID YOU KNOW?**
> In ancient times the Valley of the Kings was known as "the Great and Majestic Necropolis of the Millions of Years of the Pharaoh, Life, Strength, Health in the West of Thebes."

At least 63 tombs for pharaohs and nobles were built in the Valley of the Kings. Amenhotep I's successor, Thutmose I, who ascended to the throne around 1493 BC, is the first pharaoh known to be buried there.

THUTMOSE III ENTERS THE NETHERWORLD

The walls of the tomb of Thutmose III in the Valley of the Kings are inscribed with a long royal funerary text called the Amduat. The excerpted hieroglyphs, translated below, describe three hours of the dangerous 12-hour journey the pharaoh's soul must travel with the sun god in order to be reborn:

The first hour begins when the dying sun slips beneath the horizon. The pharaoh unites with the sun god Re and enters the netherworld on his solar boat. He is greeted by gods, goddesses, baboons, and fire-breathing serpents. . . .

Hour 7: The sun god Re confronts his archenemy, the serpent Apophis, who swallows the waters carrying the sun boat. Isis and other goddesses hurl magical spells that cut and bind Apophis, destroying his power. . . .

Hour 12: This is the hour of the sun god's rebirth. His boat is preceded by the snake known as the "World Encircler." . . . The towline held by gods and goddesses passes through the head of the snake to indicate that the sun god is pulled through the snake's body, from the tail to the mouth, and emerges rejuvenated as the scarab beetle, the sun god's morning manifestation.

Quoted in *National Geographic*, "Tomb of Thutmose III," 2012. www.nationalgeographic .com.

THEY CRAWLED ON THEIR BELLIES

Thutmose I conducted military campaigns into Nubia and Syria, but his grandson Thutmose III is remembered as one of the most daring warriors of ancient times. Thutmose III was named pharaoh around 1479 BC. After only 10 weeks on the throne he led a 10,000-man army division into battle against the Canaanites in Megiddo, a town in present-day Israel. The written records from that military action are the first reliable descriptions of Egyptian wars. They state that Thutmose III appeared on April 27, the first day of battle, dressed in shining armor and standing on a fearsome fighting chariot. His very appearance caused the enemy to retreat, as records state they "fled headlong towards Megiddo with faces of fear, abandoning their horses and their chariots of gold and silver."[16]

The large force of Egyptians surrounded the city and built a wall 7 feet (2m) high to prevent the citizens from leaving. After weeks of starvation the people of Megiddo were forced to surrender. The princes of the city crawled "on their bellies to kiss the ground to the might of his majesty, and to beg for breath for their nostrils, because of the greatness of his strength and the extent of [his] power."[17]

In the aftermath of the siege, Thutmose III conquered the entire Canaanite territory that today consists of Israel and most of Jordan. The pharaoh appointed new rulers and appropriated royal treasuries. The wine, grain, and fruits produced in the fertile fields of the Megiddo plain were confiscated and sent to Egypt along with tens of thousands of horses, sheep, cattle, and goats. Around 2,000 women and their children were taken as slaves along with the wives of the rulers. This significant victory secured Egyptian control over the region for more than 400 years.

> **DID YOU KNOW?**
> The forces of Thutmose III captured the fortified city of Joppa near modern-day Tel Aviv by secretly smuggling 200 armed soldiers into the city in large wicker baskets. At nightfall the soldiers emerged and opened the city gates to let in the army.

Thutmose III seemed to prefer fighting to living the life of a pampered pharaoh. During the next 20 years he led 16 more military campaigns, leaving his sumptuous palaces to lead his men through the dust and sand of the Middle East. Some campaigns were taken to collect riches from the princes of occupied lands, but others had stronger

Thutmose III leads his army through a mountain pass during one of his many forays into enemy territory. During his long reign as pharaoh, his military campaigns brought large areas of the Middle East and Nubia under Egyptian control.

A Soldier of Egypt Speaks

At the beginning of the Eighteenth Dynasty, a soldier named Ahmose was an officer in the Egyptian army. Ahmose left the earliest known account of Egyptian military campaigns as he described his experiences in Palestine, Nubia, and elsewhere:

I was taken to the ship "Northern," because I was brave. I followed the sovereign on foot when he rode about on his chariot. When the town of Avaris was besieged, I fought bravely on foot in his majesty's presence. Thereupon I was appointed to the ship "Rising in Memphis." . . . Then Avaris was despoiled, and I brought spoil from there: one man, three women; total, four persons. His majesty gave them to me as slaves. . . . Then I conveyed King Aakheperkare [Thutmose I], the justified, when he sailed south to Khent-hen-nefer, to crush rebellion throughout the lands, to repel the intruders from the desert region. . . . [His] majesty became enraged like a leopard. His majesty shot, and his first arrow pierced the chest of that foe. Then those [enemies turned to flee], helpless. . . . A slaughter was made among them; their dependents were carried off as living captives.

Quoted in Miriam Lichtheim, *Ancient Egyptian Literature: The New Kingdom*. Vol. 2. Berkeley and Los Angeles: University of California Press, 1976, pp. 12–13.

military objectives. For example, the fifth, sixth, and seventh campaigns of Thutmose III were conducted to annex the harbors of the city-state of Tunip in northern Syria. The ship-yards were converted into fortified military supply centers.

During more than three decades of fighting, the armies of Thutmose III captured and held large areas of the Middle East and Nubia. By the time the pharaoh died around 1425 BC, Egypt had little organized foreign opposition in the region and was at the peak of its military powers.

> **DID YOU KNOW?**
> In battle, Egyptian chariots were used as mobile combat platforms. Each carried three men: a driver and two soldiers armed with bows and arrows and stabbing spears for close-range combat.

THE TEMPLE OF AMUN

During the reign of Thutmose III a new era of public religious worship was initiated in Thebes. In previous dynasties, religious cults dedicated to various deities operated quietly or in secret. However, as Toby Wilkinson writes, during the Eighteenth Dynasty the city of Thebes "had been transformed into a giant open-air arena for the celebration of divine kingship, and the gods themselves had been brought out from behind the high walls of temples to spread their beneficence among the populous."[18]

The deity at the center of this trend was Amun, the king of all gods. Amun (also spelled Amon) was believed to be a sacred voice for the poor, silent masses. The god took on new importance during the reign of the Hyksos and was credited for helping the Egyptians conquer and expel the foreigners.

The building boom to honor Amun was initiated by Thutmose I. It was centered in what is called the Precinct of Amun-Re, a 62-acre (25ha) city of the gods filled with monuments, temples, tapered towers called pylons, and tall, narrow, four-sided, tapering monuments called obelisks. The Precinct of Amun-Re is part of the 247-acre (100ha) Karnak temple complex near ancient Thebes. Karnak exists today as four large sacred precincts, the Precinct of Mut, the Precinct of Mon-tu, and the dismantled Temple of Amenhotep IV. Only the Precinct of Amun-Re is open to visitors.

During his reign Thutmose III used the Precinct of Amun-Re to proclaim his great deeds. The walls of temples are inscribed with details of his epic battles. The black granite Victory Stele in the precinct contains 50 lines praising the pharaoh and describing how he conquered Egypt's enemies. Several towering obelisks and a large pylon were also created for this purpose.

Thutmose's most impressive addition to the precinct was his Festival Hall, built for the Heb Sed celebration. The architectural design of the building was revolutionary, with rows of columns that are tapered in reverse, larger in the middle and smaller at the ends. Legend has it that Thutmose envisioned himself spending his eternal life as a desert fighter. The columns imitate the poles of the tent he used during his many military campaigns. Behind the Festival Hall, a chamber was built with columns that represented papyrus reeds. This area is known as the Botanical Garden because it features incredible paintings of the exotic plants and animals that Thutmose brought back from Syria during the twenty-fifth year of his regency.

THE SPIRIT OF THE SUN

Amun remained the chief deity of the Eighteenth Dynasty until the reign of Amenhotep IV, which began around 1360 BC. Amenhotep was the tenth ruler of the Eighteenth Dynasty and a teenager when he ascended to the throne. Because he inherited a wealthy, stable nation at peace with its neighbors, Amenhotep was able to institute a building binge that rivaled that of previous pharaohs. But when Amenhotep ordered construction of eight new monuments in a district just outside Karnak, the move was controversial. They were built facing the sunrise in order to establish a new religion for all of Egypt and the territories beyond.

Amenhotep's red granite and sandstone temples were dedicated to the ancient sun god Aten. The pharaoh believed Aten was embodied in the rays of the sun. The pharaoh also thought Aten was the one and only god. This belief in monotheism, or a single god, was heretical to most Egyptians, who worshipped many gods. Amenhotep changed his name to Akhenaten, meaning "the Effective Spirit of Aten."

Along with his queen, Nefertiti, the pharaoh Akhenaten led a spiritual revolution. The powers of Amun, which had dominated religious belief for centuries, were diminished. Akhenaten believed he was the living incarnation of Aten, which placed the pharaoh alongside the only true god in the universe. To cement his power and spread the belief in monotheism, Akhenaten banned polytheistic beliefs. He employed teams of officials to destroy temples, statues, writings, and artwork dedicated to the hundreds of deities worshipped by the Egyptians since prehistoric times.

Akhenaten's son Tutankhamun assumed power after his father's death. Most scholars believe the boy-king Tut was guided by two powerful officials—Ay and Horemheb—who worked to undo the spread of monotheism. After Tutankhamun's death, Ay ruled for four years followed by Horemheb.

RAMESSES THE GREAT

During the religious conflict created by Akhenaten near the end of the Eighteenth Dynasty, Egypt lost control of the foreign lands captured by Thutmose III and others. By the beginning of the Nineteenth Dynasty circa 1298 BC, there was trouble in Palestine and Syria due to the growing influence of the Hittites, an ancient people native to the region. In the south the Nubians were in revolt, fighting to expel their Egyptian masters and reassert their national identity.

By the time the 24-year-old Ramesses II ascended to the throne around 1279 BC, it was necessary for Egypt to exert its military might once again in the northeast. Ramesses II assembled an army of around 100,000 warriors, a formidable force boosted by thousands of charioteers who fought in ankle-length mail (a protective metal coat). During the first decade of his reign, the pharaoh led divisions of soldiers who fought in central Africa, Libya, and Syria.

When not battling foes, Ramesses II was described as overseeing the granite quarries of Aswan, where obelisks were carved from raw stone. The pharaoh was also credited with picking out the brightest courtiers and officials to help him rule Egypt.

Ramesses II did everything on a grand scale, which earned him the title Ramesses the Great. During his 67-year reign, he was reported to have fathered 96 sons and 60 daughters with 200 wives and concubines. Some of the women were princesses from conquered territories, whom Ramesses married to join his royal house with those of his former foes. This ensured a long period of peace for Egypt.

Giant statues of Ramesses II guard the entrance to The Temple of Ramses II. Egypt enjoyed a long period of peace during his reign.

THE BUILDER

Sitting atop a mountain of gold, jewels, and other riches, Ramesses II embarked on the last great building program undertaken by the ancient Egyptians. Ramesses the Great constructed sprawling temples at Karnak and completed the Great Temple of Abydos, built to honor his father, Seti I. The memorial temple Ramesses built at Thebes, called the Ramesseum, was under construction for more than 20 years. Far to the south, in Abu Simbel in Nubia, workers carved the most famous of the pharaoh's temples from natural sandstone cliffs. The Temple of Ramesses II is guarded by four seated figures of the pharaoh, each more than 65 feet (20m) high. Statues of the ruler's favorite children are placed at his feet.

Inside the shrine eight statues of Ramesses II are attached to pillars that support the roof. These giant statues are positioned inside so that the sun shines on them only for about 20 minutes two days each year: on October 22, the pharaoh's birthday, and on February 22, the day of his coronation. To the north, another astounding shrine, the Temple of Hathor, was built to honor Ramesses's first queen, Nefertari.

Ramesses II died around 1213 BC at an estimated age of 91. Although his monuments, statues, columns, and steles are among the most dazzling of ancient Egypt, they were created at the end of an era. During the Nineteenth Dynasty, circa 1187 BC, a drought brought misery and starvation to the Egyptians. With its people in a hungry, weakened state, Egypt was overtaken by the foreigners whom Ramesses II, Thutmose III, and others had repressed for centuries. The great empire that ruled the ancient world would never again be the same.

The Foreign Rulers

During the 1100s BC the power and glory of pharaonic rule began to unravel toward the end of the Twentieth Dynasty. Eight pharaohs named Ramesses ascended to the royal throne, most for short periods. Some were remembered for their extreme corruption, but none were known to achieve greatness. The dishonest Egyptian rulers nearly bankrupted the country, leaving it vulnerable to foreign takeover.

By this time Egypt had become a magnet for immigrants who were attracted by the nation's rich culture, ancient monuments, and fertile farmlands. In nearly every city, native Egyptians conducted their daily business with Greeks, called Macedonians, as well as with Assyrians and Persians who migrated from Mesopotamia in present-day Iraq and Iran. Even Egypt's traditional enemies, the Libyans, had settled in large numbers in the western Nile delta region.

The influx of foreigners ushered in a new era for Egypt known as the Third Intermediate Period, which began around 1075 BC when the Twentieth Dynasty collapsed. For the next four centuries, until about 664 BC, Egypt was ruled by pharaohs of foreign cultures. The nation was often splintered into smaller kingdoms, ruled by warring factions in different cities.

Tasting the Taste of Piye

While the Libyans, Greeks, and Assyrians were moving into positions of power in Egypt, the Nubians were in revolt. Nubia, also called Kush, was a province of Egypt for more than five centuries. During that time, Nubia was ruled by an official called the viceroy of Kush, who reported directly to the pharaoh. Around 1070 BC the Nubians threw off Egyptian rule and founded their own independent kingdom with its capital, Napata, on the west bank of the Nile in present-day Karmia, northern Sudan.

With its location at the heart of African trade routes, the kingdom of Nubia quickly grew wealthy. Nubian rulers spent their vast treasure creating magnificent monuments, tombs, and steles that rivaled those of the Egyptians. Many of these were dedicated to the Egyptian god Amun, who the Nubians believed was the ruler of the universe.

By the mid-700s BC Egypt was fragmented and ruled by four kings, leaving the country in chaos. This prompted the Nubians to view themselves as superior to the Egyptians, who were seen as incapable of governing Egypt. The kings of Nubia believed they were the true custodians of Egypt's royal heritage. In 747 the Nubian king Piye (also spelled Piankhi) decided to invade Egypt, or as he later described it, "I shall let Lower Egypt taste the taste of my fingers."[19]

The Nubians easily conquered Thebes, and Piye named himself the first pharaoh of the Twenty-Fifth Dynasty. As Egyptologist Peter A. Clayton explains, Piye viewed the incursion "not so much as an invasion but as a restoration of the old status quo and supremacy of Amun. Hence when [Piye] moved north against the coalition of four Egyptian kings . . . he could take the view that these kings had acted like naughty children who needed to be brought into line."[20]

The New Pyramid Builders

After imposing Nubian control over Egypt, Piye returned to Napata. However, the Nubian ruler found it difficult to control a nation spread out over a 1,300 mile (2,092km) stretch of the Nile. In order to cement his power, Piye adopted the throne name Thutmose III, taken from the Eighteenth Dynasty military genius. Piye followed in Thutmose III's footsteps, ordering his army to shore up Egyptian power in the east.

One battle, described in the Bible, took place around 701 BC. It involved a large Assyrian force, led by the warrior king Esarhaddon, that conquered Judah in present-day Israel. As the Assyrians prepared to lay siege to Jerusalem, a small Nubian force approached. They were led by Piye's son, a military officer named Taharqa (sometimes spelled Taharqo). Although greatly outnumbered, the Nubian fighters rode their horses into battle against the Assyrians. The Nubians suffered many casualties, but according to scriptures, as the Jerusalemites "arose in the morning, behold, they [the Assyrian besiegers] were all dead corpses" (Isa. 37:36).

Piye also sought to imitate the Old Kingdom pyramid building boom. After visiting Giza the pharaoh became fascinated with the pyramids and began building his own along the Nile in Nubia. When Piye died around 715 BC, he was the first Egyptian pharaoh to be entombed in a pyramid in more than 800 years. Over the course of the next thousand years, the Nubians would build around 220 of their steeply walled pyramids.

> **DID YOU KNOW?**
> The pharaoh Taharqa's pyramid is the largest in Nubia, measuring about 42 feet (13m) per side at the base and rising steeply to a height of 164 feet (50m).

Many of the Nubian pyramids remain standing today. They are much smaller than those of the Old Kingdom pharaohs, consisting of a square base and walls that rise up to about 150 feet (46m) at a steep 68-degree angle. The interior walls of the Nubian pyramids are inscribed with Egyptian funerary texts, such as the Book of the Dead.

"THE ROOT OF KUSH"

Taharqa ascended to the pharaoh's throne circa 690 BC. He embarked on the greatest construction spree since Ramesses II and is remembered as one of most successful pharaohs of the era. Taharqa built

The Nubian kings believed they were the true custodians of Egypt's royal heritage. One of these foreign pharaohs, Piye, accepts the homage of a princess, as depicted in this contemporary painting.

major temples and monuments up and down the Nile from the Mediterranean to central Africa. At Karnak, Taharqa constructed many edifices to honor Amun. At the time the chief god was often depicted as a type of sphinx, with the head of a ram and the body of a lion. To show that Amun granted his kingship legitimacy, Taharqa built an avenue at Karnak and filled it with several dozen ram-headed sphinxes. The pharaoh also erected a colonnade of 10 towering granite columns at Karnak. Each slim column was around 62 feet (19m) in height and resembled a reed of papyrus. Only one column remains today; the rest were likely broken up and carried off for building materials.

LIBYAN RULERS

The Libyans who ruled Egypt between about 1069 BC and 760 BC adopted the trappings of traditional pharaonic rule. However, the Libyans did not abandon their own heritage, which was based on centuries of living in the desert as wandering nomadic tribes. With this legacy, the Libyan pharaohs governed a divided Egypt as a loose association of tribes rather than as a single central authority.

The Libyan pharaohs wore traditional feather decorations in their hair as a symbol of their ethnic origins. The pharaohs also had indigenous Libyan names, such as Takelot and Nimlot, which were foreign sounding to Egyptian ears. Perhaps most shocking to native Egyptians, the Libyans had little interest in traditions concerning death and the afterlife. As nomads, the Libyans customarily buried their dead wherever they fell. After they took control of Egypt, Libyan pharaohs viewed construction of massive tombs and temples for a single individual as a waste of resources. The Libyan pharaohs were entombed in modest communal burial vaults alongside their entire families. As a result of this practice, the construction of elaborate tombs in the Valley of the Kings came to a permanent end.

Taharqa believed his deeds pleased the gods and took personal credit for nature's bounty. During the sixth year of his reign, the Nile flooded to record levels, yielding an abundant grain harvest. To commemorate his contribution to this blessed event, Taharqa had four steles carved. The inscription on one explains that the remarkable inundation had many benefits: "It slew the rats and snakes that were in the midst of it; it kept away from it the devouring locusts. . . . I [Taharqa] reaped the harvest into barns, incalculable, even Upper Egyptian barley and Lower Egyptian barley and every seed that grows upon the surface of the earth."[21]

Taharqa's luck seemed to run out around 671 BC. The pharaoh was wounded five times during a bloody clash with the Assyrians in the Nile delta. After fighting for two weeks, the Nubians were forced to retreat to Memphis. In the aftermath, according to King Esarhaddon, the Assyrians slaughtered Egyptian villagers and "erected piles of their heads." The humiliated Taharqa fled to Nubia and never returned. As Esarhaddon stated it, "The root of Kush, I tore up out of Egypt."[22] The king captured the pharaoh's queen, harem, and heirs and carried them back to Assyria along with livestock and other riches.

> **DID YOU KNOW?**
> A stele commemorating the defeat of the Nubians in Egypt shows a picture of the Assyrian king holding a chain that pierces the tongue of his bitter enemy, the pharaoh Taharqa.

LOOTING TEMPLES AND PALACES

Taharqa continued to nominally rule Egypt from Nubia until his death circa 664 BC. Power passed to his cousin Tanutamun, who immediately organized an army to sweep north into Egypt and expel the Assyrians. The pharaoh was initially successful and reoccupied Thebes and Memphis for a few months. The Assyrians, who were known for their hard-hearted brutality, retaliated with unprecedented violence. In 664 BC they swept into Thebes and looted temples and palaces, carrying off Egyptian treasures that had accumulated over 14 centuries. The leader of the force, Assyrian king Ashurbanipal, bragged that he took

> silver, gold, precious stones, the goods of his palace, all there was, brightly colored and linen garments, great horses, the people, male and female, two tall obelisks. . . . I removed from their positions and carried them off to Assyria. Heavy plunder, and countless, I carried away from Ni' [Thebes].[23]

The Persian Conquest

The Assyrians burned Thebes as Tanutamun fled to Nubia. His death in 656 BC put a formal end to the Twenty-Fifth Dynasty. But even after the Assyrians ended Nubian domination, they could not maintain control over Egypt. After the sack of Thebes, the native Egyptian Psamtik I (also spelled Psammeticus) ascended to the throne. Psamtik was the founder of the Twenty-Sixth Dynasty, also known as the Sais Dynasty, named for the city that was the seat of power at that time.

For more than half a century Psamtik I oversaw a resurgence of ancient traditions, with artisans reviving the art and sculpture styles of the Old and Middle Kingdoms. Egypt once again prospered as foreign traders and outsiders, particularly those from Greece, poured into the country. However, a new peril threatened Egypt. To the east, the military might of Persia was growing. Beginning around 550 BC the Persian Empire extended its rule over three continents, from the modern countries of Bulgaria in southeastern Europe through Greece, Turkey, Syria, Pakistan, Afghanistan, and Saudi Arabia. In 525 BC the Persians easily conquered Egypt.

The first Persian pharaoh of the Twenty-Seventh Dynasty, Cambyses II, ruled his empire from Pasargadae, an ancient Persian city near modern Shiraz, Iran. Cambyses II took little notice of Egyptian affairs. However, his son Darius I, also known as Darius the Great, was very interested in Egypt. In the years after he ascended to the throne circa 522 BC, Darius visited Egypt three times.

Canal Construction Brings Increased Trade

One of Darius I's most ambitious projects was the construction of a canal to facilitate trade between Egypt and towns along the Persian Gulf. Darius envisioned the canal as a channel that would connect the Nile to the Red Sea, an inlet of the Indian Ocean that lies between Africa and the Middle East. This had been a dream of pharaohs since the 1800s BC, and several attempts to dig a canal had been abandoned over the centuries. One major effort by the Egyptian pharaoh Necho II failed around 600 BC. However, in an earthmoving project comparable to the construction of the Great Pyramids, Darius was able to bring the canal dream to reality. Workers dug a channel 40 miles (65km) long and 150 feet (46m) wide.

After Darius's canal opened in 497 BC, ships making the 4-day journey sailed past a series of giant pink granite steles 10 feet (3m) high and 7 feet (2m) wide. The slabs acted as billboards for Darius, with pictures and inscriptions describing his divinely inspired powers. One stele states, "I, a Persian, with Persians, I seized Egypt. I gave orders to dig a canal from the river that is in Egypt—the Nile is its name—to the bitter river [the Red Sea] that flows from Persia."[24]

> **DID YOU KNOW?**
> Herodotus wrote that Necho II's failed attempt to dig a canal connecting the Nile to the Red Sea caused 120,000 workers to perish.

THE LAST NATIVE PHARAOH

Egypt remained stable throughout the 36-year rule of Darius. However, the Persian pharaohs who followed Darius were engaged in extended wars with the Macedonian Greeks. As Persian rulers loosened their grip on Egypt, a series of native revolts created widespread anarchy. Darius's canal filled with silt, and there would be no other waterway between Egypt and the Red Sea until the Suez Canal was opened in AD 1869.

Around 404 BC Egypt regained its independence for little more than 60 years. Nectanebo II, who reigned from 360 to 343 BC, was the last Egyptian pharaoh. The Persians returned and ruled for about nine years. By this time Egypt was a nation of 8 million people who could no longer rely on their ancient traditions, riches, or religion to remain free. As Egyptologist Toby Wilkinson writes, "Egypt had lost

THE CROWN JEWEL OF ALEXANDRIA

Alexander the Great founded 70 cities on three continents, but Alexandria, Egypt, was the crown jewel of them all. Alexander laid out the city in a grid pattern with wide boulevards intersecting at right angles. Within a century of its founding, the city was the second largest in the world, after Rome. As the capital of Egypt, about one-third of Alexandria was dominated by dazzling royal places, monuments, government buildings, courts, schools, and sports facilities. The most sensational of the polished granite and marble buildings in Alexandria was the Royal Library. The impressive library was founded by Ptolemy I and was expanded by successive pharaohs. By 250 BC the library contained an estimated half a million papyrus scrolls on physics, mathematics, philosophy, religion, medicine, and almost every other imaginable subject.

As a center of learning, the Royal Library of Alexandria was a magnet for Greek intellectuals whose work profoundly influenced Western culture. The mathematician Euclid worked there, as did the engineer Archimedes. The astronomer Aristarchus of Samos relied on the scrolls to devise his theory of the solar system with the Sun at its center. The Royal Library was eventually destroyed, although the exact time and method is unknown. However, by the early centuries AD the center of all ancient knowledge had disappeared forever, along with half a million priceless scrolls and books.

its preeminence and was now just another country—albeit a wealthy one—to be fought over by younger, nimbler empires. . . . Frightened and bewildered by the rapidly changing global situation, most Egyptians preferred to look the other way, put their trust in the old gods, and carry on."[25]

ALEXANDER THE GREAT

The Persian occupation of Egypt ended in 332 BC, when the Macedonian king Alexander the Great defeated the Persian army. Alexander is one of the most celebrated military geniuses in history. He became king of Greece in 336 BC at the age of 20, and during the next several years Alexander built an empire that stretched across three continents. The Macedonians swept east to conquer all the lands between Europe and Tibet, including the Levant, Syria, Egypt, Assyria, Persia, and India.

When Alexander rode into Memphis in 332 BC, the Egyptians welcomed him as a liberator, someone who freed them from nearly two centuries of despised Persian rule. Alexander lived up to the expectations of the Egyptians, holding ceremonies to celebrate the Egyptian gods and goddesses of old. Alexander was only in Egypt for four months, but he made a lasting impact on the nation. Before he left he laid out a new capital that he named Alexandria. Alexander designed Alexandria carefully. He chose a site 20 miles (32km) from the Mediterranean with natural deepwater harbors. This allowed for the construction of wharves, warehouses, and shipyards that quickly made Alexandria a major naval port, trading hub, and political and cultural center. Even as the first foundations of Alexandria were laid, Alexander rode off to conquer Persia. He fought on for 10 more years but died from malaria in Babylon in 323 BC. He was 32 years old.

> **DID YOU KNOW?**
> The Egyptian economy was based on barter until the Greeks introduced money in the form of coins during the early 400s BC.

PHAROS

Alexander the Great spent little time in Egypt but he left behind plans for a new capital that would become a thriving economic, political, and cultural center. The world's first lighthouse, the Pharos of Alexandria (pictured), was built in the city's harbor after Alexander's death.

THE PTOLEMIES

Alexander's vast empire was divided between his generals. Ptolemy, the son of one of Alexander's seven bodyguards, became pharaoh of Egypt and founded the Ptolemaic Dynasty. Ptolemy's son, Ptolemy II, was known for his lavish and extreme parties. The pharaoh celebrated his accession in 285 BC with a huge party and parade that featured more than 100,000 people, barrels of wine, mountains of food, and a cavalcade of dancers, acrobats, and exotic animals. The party would have cost millions of dollars in modern times and was part of the outrageous excesses of a dynasty whose deeds soon turned dark and ugly.

Writer Chip Brown explains, "The Ptolemies of Macedonia are one of history's most flamboyant dynasties, famous not only for wealth and wisdom but also for bloody rivalries and the sort of 'family values' that modern-day exponents of the phrase would surely disavow, seeing as they included incest and fratricide."[26]

During the Ptolemaic Dynasty, which endured until 30 BC, many Egyptians adopted Greek speech, dress, and culture as their own. In return, the Greeks borrowed from the ancient Egyptians, particularly their religious beliefs. This melding of art, philosophy, and science would influence European and Western culture for centuries.

> **DID YOU KNOW?**
> Alexander the Great founded 20 cities that bore his name, including Alexandria, Egypt.

CHAPTER 5

Women of
the Crown

Life and death in ancient Egypt closely revolved around the rise
and fall of the Nile, the passing of the seasons, and the rhythms
of the Sun, the Moon, and the planets. Egyptian religion was centered
on the forces of nature ruled by female deities, including Isis, Hathor,
Maat, and other goddesses. Archaeologist Joann Fletcher describes
Egypt as "a culture that believed the whole universe was a balance of
male and female, a duality which was essential for the continuity of
life and gave balance to all things. And the very symbol of cosmic order was a female deity, Maat, whose presence prevented the forces of
chaos from overwhelming the order that only she could maintain."[27]

Because of this belief women played a large role in Egyptian religion. One of the most common careers for women during pharaonic
times was the priesthood, and nearly every temple had a high priestess.
Women acted alongside men at religious festivals, ceremonies, funer-
als, and other events.

The status women enjoyed in religious matters carried over to other
aspects of Egyptian society. Women had the same legal and economic
rights as men, according to ancient manuscripts. Egyptian women
could sign a variety of contracts and buy and sell private property,
including slaves, land, livestock, and servants. This situation was very
different in Greece, where women had few rights. Describing Egypt in
440 BC, Herodotus was shocked upon seeing women "attending mar-

ket and taking part in trading whereas men sat at home and did the weaving.... [The] Egyptians themselves in their manner and customs seem to have reversed the ordinary practices of mankind."[28]

In addition to trading, women were shown in artistic depictions working as sailors, farmers, artisans, and laborers. And although the majority of government officials were men, women served in Egypt's vast bureaucracy as overseers, governors, and judges. Two women were viziers, or prime ministers, the most powerful office below that of pharaoh. Although ancient Egypt was a moneyless society, ancient records show that working women were paid with the same trade goods, livestock, and rations of grain, beer, and vegetables as men.

THE KING'S MOTHER

Most Egyptian women were wives and mothers, and one of the most important titles in ancient Egypt was *mwt nswt,* or "the king's mother." This title was given to the pharaoh's senior wife, who was also the queen. Although pharaohs had many wives, and some were more important than others, there was only one queen. Her main duty was to provide the pharaoh with many children, especially male heirs.

Lives were short in ancient times, and pharaohs often died when their sons were too young to serve. In such cases the king's mother was named a coregent, ruling as a pharaoh until the designated heir was old enough to take over. Sometimes a king's mother acted as pharaoh for an extended period.

The first known mother of a king to assume the role of coregent was Merneith. She was the senior wife of Djet, a First Dynasty pharaoh. When Djet died, Merneith ruled as a coregent for an unknown length of time with her son Den. When Merneith died she was buried in Abydos. Her tomb is as large as those of the other pharaohs, indicating she was of equal status. In addition, a royal seal found in Den's tomb includes the name Merneith on a register of First Dynasty kings.

The mother of the Old Kingdom's Sixth Dynasty pharaoh Pepi II, named Ankhesenpepi II, also ruled as a coregent. Pepi was only about six years old when he became pharaoh. One of the only three known images of Pepi is a small alabaster statue that depicts the young boy in full pharaonic regalia sitting on Ankhesenpepi's lap.

Nitocris Drowns Her Enemies

Pepi II is said to have ruled for at least 90 years. After his long reign, Egypt was faced with a crisis over succession. His son was already very old, and his reign lasted only about one year. The gender of Egypt's next pharaoh, Neitiqerty Siptah, is shrouded in mystery. The pharaoh's name references the female war deity Neith, whose symbol was a shield crossed with arrows. Both Manetho and Herodotus referred to Neitiqerty Siptah by the Greek name Nitocris. Herodotus says Nitocris was a woman who ascended to the throne upon the murder of her brother, whom he fails to name. Although her anonymous brother's enemies proceeded to make her pharaoh, Nitocris avenged his death with an elaborate plot in which they were drowned in the waters of the Nile. According to Herodotus,

> [Nitocris] constructed a very large chamber under ground, and . . . she invited those of the Egyptians whom she knew to have had most part in the murder, and gave a great banquet. Then while they were feasting, she let in the river upon them by a secret conduit of large size. . . . [When] this had been accomplished, she threw herself into a room full of embers, [committing suicide] in order that she might escape vengeance.[29]

The Pharaoh's Regalia

Some Egyptologists doubt that Nitocris really existed since there is scant proof other than writings created several millennia after her

WOMEN OF VIOLENCE

Female Egyptian deities were known for violence and destruction. It was believed the war goddess Neith could destroy the world by making the sky collapse. Sekhmet, whose name means "Powerful Female," was an astonishing beauty who could turn into a killer lioness on a moment's notice. In this form she hunted humans for sport, earning a second name—the Lady of the Red Linen—that symbolized the blood-soaked clothing of her slaughtered enemies. As archaeologist Joann Fletcher writes, mortal Egyptian women were also known for their fierce deeds:

> The Egyptian acknowledgment of the female capacity for violence was not . . . restricted to goddesses. In a range of artistic representations, female town dwellers stab invading male soldiers, a female pharaoh fires arrows at a male opponent, Hatshepsut carries a mace when still a queen, [the royal wife] Tiy attacks the enemy as a sphinx, and Nefertiti executes prisoners with her scimitar. . . . Some women were threatening enough to be listed as enemies of the state; Hatshepsut is named "She Who Will Be a Conqueror"; whilst the earlier Queen Ahhotep rallied Egypt's troops and was buried with full military honors and splendid weapons. Indeed, stone maces and daggers have been discovered in female graves dating back to . . . 3100 BC.

Joann Fletcher, *The Search for Nefertiti: The True Story of an Amazing Discovery.* New York: William Morrow, 2004, p. 192.

purported reign. This is not true in the case of Queen Sobekneferu (also written as Nefrusobek), whose reign is documented in ancient texts and artwork. Sobekneferu was the royal daughter of the pharaoh Amenemhat III, who came to power near the end of the Middle Kingdom's Twelfth Dynasty.

One life-size sculpture depicts Sobekneferu in female clothing but wearing the regalia of a male pharaoh, including a kilt and a striped head cloth called a *nemes*. In addition, her name is written on her belt buckle in the manner of male pharaohs. Another sculpture shows Sobekneferu in a man's coronation cloak and a headdress that features the pharaonic symbol of two vultures surrounding a protective cobra.

Sobekneferu's rule was short, slightly less than four years, but her name lives on at one of Egypt's most amazing mortuary temples. Sobekneferu's father initiated construction at the remarkable pyramid complex at Hawara, which was called the labyrinth by Herodotus. The structure features hundreds of underground rooms and galleries—Herodotus put their number at 3,000—connected by intricate maze-like passageways. The roofs, floors, and walls are all exquisite white marble and are filled with carvings of countless figures. The labyrinth ends at Amenemhat III's pyramid, which rises 240 feet (73m) above the courtyard. The pharaoh died before his pyramid was completed, but his devoted daughter Sobekneferu finished the structure. In the royal tradition, Sobekneferu's name was carved into every block laid on the pyramid, making her inscriptions more numerous than her father's. The female pharaoh later oversaw construction of her own pyramid south of Dahshur.

HATSHEPSUT GOVERNED THE LAND

The queen of all ancient Egyptian queens, Hatshepsut, was the daughter, wife, and possibly the granddaughter of pharaohs. She became pharaoh during the Eighteenth Dynasty, circa 1473 BC, but she had a

Hatshepsut, the female pharaoh who ruled Egypt for about 20 years, left a legacy in stone. A colossal statue of Hatshepsut, wearing the symbol of pharaonic power—the false beard—guards her tomb at Deir el-Bahri near the Valley of the Kings.

circuitous path to the throne. Hatshepsut's rise to power began when her father, Thutmose I, died without producing a male heir with his principal wife, Ahmose. The pharaoh did have a son, Thutmose II, who was born to a secondary wife. Before Thutmose II could be crowned pharaoh sometime around 1493 BC, he needed to have a stronger tie to the royal bloodline. In typical pharaonic style, he entered into an arranged marriage with the fully royal Hatshepsut, his half sister who was probably a teenager at the time.

It is unclear how old Thutmose II was at the time of his marriage, but as a royal heiress Hatshepsut was able to take advantage of her position. She had herself named "god's wife of Amun," an important religious and political title that made her the highest-ranking priestess in the powerful Amun cult.

Like his father, Thutmose II fathered only a daughter with his wife. The pharaoh's son and heir, Thutmose III, was produced with a secondary wife, Isis. Thutmose II died soon after his son was born, sometime around 1479 BC, and the infant Thutmose was named coregent with Hatshepsut, his stepmother. According to ancient texts, however, Hatshepsut ruled alone: "[She] governed the land, and the Two Lands [Upper and Lower Egypt] were under her control; people work for her, and Egypt bowed the head."[30]

Like Sobekneferu, Hatshepsut dressed in male regalia. She appeared at events wearing a man's crown, kilt, and scepter. She even tied on the traditional false beard. Reliefs made at the time show the queen in a kilt, striding forward and reaching out as a king would do. This differed from conventional art, which showed female figures standing passively, arms at their sides, feet together, and legs covered with ankle-length dresses. Reliefs also showed Hatshepsut performing rituals that had been conducted by male pharaohs for hundreds of years. They include making offerings, celebrating festivals, spearing fish in marshes, trampling foes, and beating enemies over the head.

A LONG, PROSPEROUS REIGN

Unlike previous female pharaohs whose reigns lasted only briefly, Hatshepsut maintained power for about 20 years. She followed the policies of previous pharaohs, maintaining Egypt's sprawling empire. Ancient texts state that she captured rebel chiefs in Palestine and sent the army to Nubia, where towns were pillaged and foes were slaughtered. The queen sent workers into the Sinai to mine turquoise and copper and imported great quantities of fragrant frankincense and myrrh from Punt, a mythical land said to have been located on the Red Sea coast.

Egypt prospered under Hatshepsut's rule, and she used the kingdom's wealth to build a tremendous funerary temple. It was located on the west bank of the Nile beneath the cliffs at Deir el-Bahri near the Valley of the Kings. Like so many pharaohs before her, Hatshepsut used this shrine to proclaim her divine family heritage. On a series of wall panels at her temple, Hatshepsut claims she is the daughter of Amun. Her divine birth was a result of the night her mother, Ahmose, spent with Amun, who disguised himself as the pharaoh. The final panel in the story shows Queen Ahmose holding the infant Hatshepsut in front of four goddesses who acted as midwives. The inscription immodestly states that

> [Hatshepsut] became more important than anyone else. What was within her was godlike; godlike was everything she did; her spirit was godlike. Her majesty became a beautiful maiden, blossoming out. The goddess Uto, at this moment, applauded her divine shapeliness. She is a woman of distinguished appearance.[31]

Hatshepsut was one of ancient Egypt's most productive builders, and her temples and monuments can be seen today throughout Egypt. One of her major projects stands at Karnak, across the Nile from her funerary temple. The queen enlarged the Precinct of Mut and installed two of the tallest obelisks in the world. One remains standing, but the other broke in half and fell to the ground.

HATSHEPSUT'S DEATH

When Hatshepsut's trusted adviser, Senmut, died around 1462 BC, she reinstated Thutmose III as a coregent. On one scene at a Karnak temple, the two are depicted wearing identical crowns and kilts, both holding a king's scepter in their right hands. Although the date of Hatshepsut's birth is unknown, she was probably no older than 45 when she died during the twenty-second year of her reign around 1458 BC. There is speculation that Thutmose III poisoned her so he could finally become the sole pharaoh of Egypt. This remains unproved, but there was a concerted effort to destroy any mention of Hatshepsut's reign in the decades after her death. Her images and inscriptions were chiseled off temple walls. At Deir el-Bahri dozens of statues of the queen were disfigured, dumped into a quarry, and buried. At Karnak there was a failed attempt to build walls around the giant obelisks she erected.

Egyptologists speculate that Thutmose III was trying to rewrite history by removing Hatshepsut from the royal record. However, Fletcher believes Thutmose III held no animosity toward his stepmother and the destruction was undertaken by "the puritanical kings of the 19th dynasty who did the same to monuments of Akhenaten and Nefertiti."[32] Whatever the case, no one could erase the fact that Hatshepsut was the longest-reigning female pharaoh in Egyptian history.

THE LAST QUEEN OF THE NILE

Hatshepsut might have held great powers, but her fame pales next to ancient Egypt's last reigning queen, Cleopatra VII. Unlike previous queens, Cleopatra was not Egyptian. She was descended from the long line of Greeks whose Ptolemaic rulers had governed Egypt for nearly three centuries. The story of her rise and fall constitutes one of the greatest dramas of the ancient world.

Cleopatra was 18 years old when her father, Ptolemy XII, died in 51 BC. In his will Ptolemy XII named Cleopatra a coregent along with her 10-year-old brother Ptolemy XIII. To ensure the strength of the royal bond, Cleopatra and her brother were married. Early in Cleopatra's reign drought and famine brought great suffering to Egypt. People came to believe the gods had deserted Cleopatra, and the drought was her fault. Public opinion turned to favor her brother, and by 48 BC relations between Cleopatra and Ptolemy XIII had shattered. Both raised armies that fought one another in a bloody civil war. Cleopatra lost and was temporarily banished from Egypt.

During this era Egyptian rulers were forced to provide food and pay taxes to the Roman Empire, which was much more powerful and influential than Egypt. This was meant to keep the Romans from invad-

Julius Caesar leads Cleopatra back to the throne of Egypt, as depicted in this seventeenth-century painting. Cleopatra came to power with Caesar's help and gained acceptance as Egypt's rightful pharaoh, but she also has the distinction of being Egypt's last pharaoh.

ing Egypt. Cleopatra came to believe she could return to the throne if she enlisted the help of the 52-year-old Roman general Julius Caesar. Cleopatra offered to supply Caesar's army with grain and ships in exchange for his military support. To seal the deal she became Caesar's mistress.

In 47 BC Caesar ordered Roman soldiers to destroy Ptolemy XIII's forces. The pharaoh was captured and drowned in the Nile. Although Cleopatra triumphed over her brother, Egyptians were the losers. Four hundred Roman troop ships sailed up the Nile, and the Roman legions took control of Alexandria. To prevent a rebellion against her rule, Cleopatra tried to make amends. She embraced ancient pharaonic traditions, dedicated a temple to the goddess Hathor, and promoted the cult of Isis, one of the most popular Egyptian deities of the time. Cleopatra took to appearing in public in the holy dress of Isis and also adopted a Horus name. By choosing a Horus name, Cleopatra indicated she revered and respected one of the oldest symbols of divine rule.

Many Egyptians came to accept Cleopatra as their rightful pharaoh, but she soon left her kingdom. In 47 BC the queen had a child with Caesar named Caesarion, or "Little Caesar." The following year she traveled to Rome, where she lived with Caesar for two years until he was assassinated on March 15, 44 BC. Within a month Cleopatra returned to Egypt, where she elevated her three-year-old son, Caesarion, to pharaoh, renaming him Ptolemy XV.

DEATH AND IMMORTALITY

Cleopatra still needed Roman support to maintain her rule, so she formed an alliance with Mark Antony, another powerful general. The two were married in 37 BC, and together they had three children. Antony and Cleopatra worked to set up a vast Roman-Egyptian empire that they hoped would be ruled by their sons someday. However, the Roman leader Octavian had other plans.

> **DID YOU KNOW?**
> Between AD 1540 and 2011 the deeds of Cleopatra provided inspiration for five ballets, 45 operas, 77 plays, and at least seven movies, prompting critic Harold Bloom to call the queen the world's first celebrity.

Octavian overthrew Mark Antony and seized power in Rome in 31 BC. Cleopatra sought to establish a relationship with him, but her offers were refused. The Romans conquered Egypt in 30 BC, forcing the defeated Antony to flee to Alexandria. Antony mistakenly thought Cleopatra had committed suicide. He was so saddened by this that he killed himself, falling on the blade of his sword. Ten days later the last queen of Egypt was about to be arrested by Octavian's men. Legend has it that Cleopatra allowed herself to be bitten by an asp (cobra). The venom killed her.

In ancient Egypt the asp was said to be the minister of the sun god. The bite of the asp was thought to bestow immortality and divinity. Whether or not Cleopatra was actually bitten by an asp, she certainly was immortalized. For more than 400 years after her death,

NEFERTITI

The name Nefertiti means "the Beautiful One Who Has Come" in Egyptian. And although ancient paintings show Nefertiti to be a great beauty, she was also a powerful queen, married to Akhenaten, the Eighteenth Dynasty pharaoh. Akhenaten created controversy by promoting the heretical concept of a single god, Aten. Nefertiti was the pharaoh's partner in this religious reformation, which began around 1350 BC. Around 1340 BC Akhenaten announced Nefertiti's new position as coregent. In the aftermath, Nefertiti was depicted in poses and regalia only used by male pharaohs.

After only two years as coregent, Nefertiti disappeared from view. Some believe she split with Akhenaten and was banished from the royal palace. Others think Nefertiti adopted the man's name Smenkhkare and continued to rule as coregent with her husband. The conventional view is that the queen died from the plague epidemic that was sweeping through the kingdom at the time. Today an ancient lifelike bust of Nefertiti resides in Berlin's Neues Museum, providing a haunting image of a mysterious female pharaoh from long ago.

Cleopatra was worshipped by a religious cult in Rome. Her life has been dramatized by playwright William Shakespeare and portrayed in film by Elizabeth Taylor.

Cleopatra's son by Caesar, King Ptolemy XV, was murdered at the age of 17 by Octavian's forces. The Romans were now in control of Egypt, and the age of the pharaohs was over. After 3,100 years, the ancient hieroglyphic phrase *ankh djet,* or "living forever," could no longer be applied to pharaohs of Egypt.

SOURCE NOTES

INTRODUCTION: THE DIVINE RULER

1. Toby Wilkinson, *The Rise and Fall of Ancient Egypt*. New York: Random House, 2010, p. 28.
2. Quoted in Wilkinson, *The Rise and Fall of Ancient Egypt*, p. 26.

CHAPTER ONE: THE FOUNDING PHARAOHS

3. Quoted in Alan Gardiner, *Egypt of the Pharaohs*. London: Oxford University Press, 1964, p. 27.
4. Quoted in Cyril Aldred, *Egypt to the End of the Old Kingdom*. New York: McGraw-Hill, 1965, p. 45.
5. Quoted in Wilkinson, *The Rise and Fall of Ancient Egypt*, p. 23.
6. John Galvin, "Abydos," *National Geographic*, April 2005. http://ngm.nationalgeographic.com.
7. Wilkinson, *The Rise and Fall of Ancient Egypt*, p. 38.
8. Quoted in Peter A. Clayton, *Chronicle of the Pharaohs*. New York: Thames and Hudson, 1994, p. 24.
9. Wilkinson, *The Rise and Fall of Ancient Egypt*, p. 38.

CHAPTER TWO: THE MONUMENT BUILDERS

10. Clayton, *Chronicle of the Pharaohs*, p. 37.
11. Wilkinson, *The Rise and Fall of Ancient Egypt*, p. 55.
12. Wilkinson, *The Rise and Fall of Ancient Egypt*, p. 58.
13. Herodotus, *An Account of Egypt*. Rockville, MD. 2008, p. 64.

CHAPTER THREE: PHARAOHS OF THE GOLDEN EMPIRE

14. Howard Carter, *The Tomb of Tutankhamun*. Washington, DC: National Geographic Adventure Classics, 2003, p. 38.
15. Carter, *The Tomb of Tutankhamun*, p. 3.

16. Quoted in Miriam Lichtheim, *Ancient Egyptian Literature: The New Kingdom*, vol. 2. Berkeley and Los Angeles: University of California Press, 1976, p. 32.

17. Quoted in Lichtheim, *Ancient Egyptian Literature*, p. 33.

18. Wilkinson, *The Rise and Fall of Ancient Egypt*, p. 225.

CHAPTER FOUR: THE FOREIGN RULERS

19. Quoted in Robert Draper, "The Black Pharaohs," *National Geographic*, February 2008. http://ngm.nationalgeographic.com.

20. Clayton, *Chronicle of the Pharaohs*, pp. 190–91.

21. Quoted in Nicolås Grimal, *A History of Ancient Egypt*. Malden, MA: Blackwell, p. 347.

22. Quoted in Draper, "The Black Pharaohs."

23. Quoted in Richard D. Patterson, *Nahum, Habakkuk, Zephaniah—an Exegetical Commentary*. Richardson, TX: Biblical Studies, 2003, p. 92.

24. Quoted in Wilkinson, *The Rise and Fall of Ancient Egypt*, p. 426.

25. Wilkinson, *The Rise and Fall of Ancient Egypt*, p. 439.

26. Chip Brown, "Cleopatra," *National Geographic*, July 2011. http://ngm.nationalgeographic.com.

CHAPTER FIVE: WOMEN OF THE CROWN

27. Joann Fletcher, *The Search for Nefertiti: The True Story of an Amazing Discovery*. New York: William Morrow, 2004, p. 187.

28. Quoted in Fletcher, *The Search for Nefertiti*, p. 193.

29. Herodotus, *An Account of Egypt*, p. 50.

30. Quoted in Leonard Cottrell, *Lady of the Two Lands: Five Queens of Ancient Egypt*. Indianapolis: Bobbs-Merrill, 1967, p. 30.

31. Quoted in Cottrell, *Lady of the Two Lands*, p. 36.

32. Fletcher, *The Search for Nefertiti*, p. 220.

FOR FURTHER RESEARCH

Books

Stuart A. Kallen, *Ancient Egypt.* San Diego: ReferencePoint, 2012.

Don Nardo, *Ancient Egyptian Art and Architecture.* Farmington Hills, MI: Lucent, 2011.

James Putnam, *Pyramid.* New York: Dorling Kindersley, 2011.

Vicky Alvear Shecter, *Cleopatra Rules! The Amazing Life of the Original Teen Queen.* Honesdale, PA: Boyds Mills, 2010.

John H. Taylor, *Spells for Eternity: The Ancient Egyptian Book of the Dead.* London: British Museum, 2010.

Joyce Tyldesley, *Tutankhamen: The Search for an Egyptian King.* New York: Basic, 2012.

Websites

Discovering Ancient Egypt (www.eyelid.co.uk). A colorful British site designed to provide maximum information about all aspects of ancient Egypt. It has complete listings of dynasties and pharaohs as well as links to maps, graphs, photos, and videos. The site also features dozens of animations that provide tours of temples, tombs, and even a pharaoh's funeral procession.

Egypt: Secrets of the Ancient World (www.nationalgeographic.com /pyramids). This interactive site hosted by National Geographic contains photos, videos, and maps about ancient Egypt as well as news stories about the latest fascinating archaeological discoveries.

Giza Archives (www.gizapyramids.org). This comprehensive site hosted by Boston's Museum of Fine Arts contains thousands of photographs, maps, digitized articles, and records of tomb, monument, and object excavations. They have been compiled from the Giza excavation conducted between 1902 and 1947. The site also features more than 1,000 panoramic views of the site on Quick Time Virtual Reality.

Guardian's Egypt (http://guardians.net/egypt). One of the oldest ancient Egyptian sites, this one highlights photos of monuments and tombs and features interviews with archaeologists and antiquities experts.

King Tut (www.king-tut.org.uk). This extensive British site starts with short paragraphs and bullet points about Egypt's most famous pharaoh and provides links to dozens of pages featuring quick reference points about deities, mummies, tombs, various kingdoms and periods, and other pharaohs.

KingTutOne (www.kingtutone.com). A site with biographies of some of the most famous pharaohs, including Akhenaten, Amenhotep III, Cleopatra, Hatshepsut, Khufu, and Tutankhamun. There are links to pages about the pyramids, temples, mummies, and gods and even a game page.

Zahi Hawass (www.drhawass.com). The homepage of world-renowned archaeologist Zahi Hawass, who served as secretary general of the Supreme Council of Antiquities and directed excavations at Giza, Saqqara, and in the Valley of the Kings. This site features the latest news concerning discoveries in Egypt.

INDEX

ABOUT THE AUTHOR

Stuart A. Kallen is the author of more than 250 nonfiction books for children and young adults. He has written on topics ranging from the theory of relativity to the history of rock and roll. In addition, Kallen has written award-winning children's video and television scripts. In his spare time he is a singer/songwriter/guitarist in San Diego.